Laura M. Starin

A Trip to Europe

Being some Account of the Wanderings of a small Family Party

Laura M. Starin

A Trip to Europe
Being some Account of the Wanderings of a small Family Party

ISBN/EAN: 9783337143923

Printed in Europe, USA, Canada, Australia, Japan

Cover: Foto ©ninafisch / pixelio.de

More available books at **www.hansebooks.com**

A TRIP TO EUROPE.

BEING SOME ACCOUNT OF

THE WANDERINGS

OF A

SMALL FAMILY PARTY.

NEW YORK:
MARTIN B. BROWN, PRINTER AND STATIONER,
Nos. 49 and 51 Park Place.
1868.

ERRATA.

Page 36—Read Louis XV. for Louis XIV.

Page 59—Read Ariadne for Adrienne; also, Dannerker for Daneneker.

I.

A Plan Long Cherished.

To my husband, children and grandchildren, I dedicate this little work. It is written without desire for self-seeking, and certainly not intended for the public eye. The preparation of the notes which follow has been a labor of love with me—such a labor because I have hoped that, in living with me over again scenes and incidents which are cherished by me, those who are nearest and dearest might also find interest and pleasure.

For a long time prior to its fruition the trip, of which I am about to write, had been a matter of discussion in the family circle. My husband had been to Europe two years before, leaving me in charge of our affairs, and feeling better satisfied with doing so than for both to be absent from home and country at the same time. To us, who had not been to Europe, it seemed a great undertaking and a dangerous one—he felt thus (he has since crossed the ocean four times), and so I felt. It required consideration as well as courage to leave husband, home, children and an aged mother.

Our arrangements included my daughter Caroline's closing our city house and going to "Starin Place," Fultonville, taking charge of the establishment with her two children, three of her sisters with their maids, and her own servants, for the summer—no small undertaking for one so young. I had previously been to "Starin Place," to bid my mother good-bye, no easy task—as she so depends upon me—arrange the house for occupancy, etc. The night before I left, my friends and neighbors and pastor called to express their kindly interest and good will; prayer was offered, and we parted in tears and sadness—it being far from a joyous "surprise party"—though nothing but the best intentions were designed.

All preliminaries being settled, our passage engaged sometime in advance, a party of three, consisting of my daughter Harriet and her husband, James D. Spraker, and myself, started for a European trip of two months or more duration, as circumstances might determine. On Wednesday, June 3, 1885, at eight o'clock in the morning, we drove to the dock of the Anchor line Steamship Company and went on board the fine ship "City of Rome," bound for Liverpool, my husband and all my children accompanying me with other friends to bid us adieu and wish us "bon voyage." Some tears were shed, yet I felt more composed at parting than I had supposed possible ; hope and anticipation buoyed me up, together with a firm trust in an overruling Providence, which had for so many years been my shield and comfort. Before our friends left the ship we all went on a tour of inspection, visiting our staterooms, where we were to spend the next week, finding our steamer chairs, robes, wraps, every comfort as well as luxury. Here was an immense basket of fruit, rich and rare, seasonable and unseasonable, such as luscious hot-house grapes, oranges, lemons, bananas, apples, peaches, pears and plums, figs also, the gift of my generous husband. Charles and Ida also contributed a basket with similar contents. After inspecting all this, with just appreciation of the bounty and thoughtful kindness, the party went to the dining hall, where long tables were covered with flowers in profusion, the gifts of friends the travelers were leaving. What was our surprise to find several large baskets, with cards attached, for Harriet and myself, one for each of us from her father ; mine was three feet high, filled with large roses, Jacqueminots and other roses, pink, and white, with mignonette, great clusters of snowball hanging from sides of it.

Caroline also gave her sister and me a very large, handsome basket of flowers, as well as each a fine box of Huyler's best and rarest candy, containing our favorite kind. I also received one from Mr. Egerton, a valued and long trusted employee and friend of my husband and the family. A floral ship was given Harriet, named after her daughters Laura Belle and Daisy, from her husband's gentlemen friends. Mr. Simon presented each of us with large bouquets of roses. After admiring all these testimonials of love and friendship we went on deck, as the time was drawing near for the last good-bye and for the visitors to leave the pilgrims and the ship. After this the great vessel began to move, at first so slowly that it was hardly perceptible, amid the waving of handkerchiefs, etc. We gazed on the loved ones we were leaving with sadness, realizing all that might happen during our absence, and we continued to gaze until lost to sight and we were left to our fate.

This June day was bright and beautiful; nothing but parting with dear friends in view of a somewhat prolonged absence and the perils of an ocean voyage occurred to mar our pleasure. Never was there a party that set out for a tour under more auspicious circumstances—so favored with the prayers and good wishes of many friends.

II.

A Week at Sea.

Well, we steamed out to sea. Many, before reaching Sandy Hook, were busy with pens and portfolios. I could not understand why, until later I learned they were sending back messages to friends just parted from, by the pilot boat, which leaves the ship at this point. Very soon the last vestige of land was lost to sight—nothing but sky and water visible, and we were on the broad Atlantic ocean. We sat huddled together on deck in our steamer chairs, indispensable comforts that had been provided for us with warm robes, also necessary, talking of the incidents of the morning, of the parting, not in a very gay or festive mood. Thus the first day passed. Not mingling with our fellow-passengers, we were a community alone. The ocean was as calm as a river and the steamer glided quietly along.

The "City of Rome" is the second largest ship in the world, the "Great Eastern" only being larger. The "City of Rome" is 560 feet long. making an immense promenade of which most of the passengers avail themselves, walking as if for wagers. Thus passed the first day out very quietly; no sickness. But while sitting on deck the second day I was suddenly attacked by a slight sickness. I went to my stateroom and slept it off; in fact the strong sea air made me very sleepy. I surprised Harriet and James by walking into the dining-room at six o'clock P. M. to dinner, luncheon this day being the only meal I had missed so far—Harriet and James none.

JUNE 5TH—FRIDAY.—Capt. Munro has just been talking with us, and says to-morrow at daybreak, we may look for icebergs and fog. He dreads it (the latter), as on crossing the ocean the time before this trip, on the banks of Newfoundland, the ship, in a dense fog, ran into and sunk a French bark anchored at that point; only two lives saved (two men); twenty-two lost. At noon to-day we shall be 800 miles from New York. Our staterooms are light and airy, outside rooms commodious, with good beds, electric-lights, running water in basins, good attendance from stewards; altogether we are traveling in royal style over the trackless ocean.

With naught but sky and water to be seen on Friday evening, a rain-storm set in; the wind had been blowing pretty hard for 24 hours, yet I am not afraid. The ship rocks, the wind and waves roar; the ship seems so large and staunch that it allays fear; the wind favors a quick passage; all sails are set. I am writing on deck in my steamer chair, the wind blowing a gale. Harriet and I both have our sealskin cloaks on for comfort. Friday eve, we had a sample of Old Ocean in a storm, though not a severe one.

SATURDAY, 6TH.—Three icebergs have been seen this morning, about 10½ o'clock; others were seen earlier; more are expected; the sun shines brightly; the air is clear and cold. All were interested—of course, a sight not often seen. At first the berg only looked like a white cloud on the horizon. It became larger speedily, and soon, with the aid of opera-glasses, looked like the outlines of a castle—two large towers joined together with a large body of ice attached to the rear, thus simulating a castle in breadth as well as height, glistening in the sun. The air grew chilly, though the sun shone brightly. It was an immense iceberg of clear ice, with some snow on top, apparently, and on one end. The captain informed us that it was 500 feet long and 80 feet high—truly a wonderful sight. Eight bergs seen this day at a distance. The large one described was about a quarter of a mile distant.

MONDAY.—We have experienced a storm at sea since Saturday last; nearly all on board the ship were sick; only one or two ladies in dining-room. Harriet and I both sick; James, not at all. We were quite comfortable in our staterooms, and in our berths all day and night. Stewardess was very kind, and everything that a first-class hotel affords was at our command. The vessel rocked so that we could hardly stay in our berths; the waves dashed against the portholes fearfully; the phosphorescent light through the waves was a wonderful sight, like brilliant stars or like tongues of fire breaking against the thick glass of the portholes; how furiously the waters dashed and lashed themselves into white foam—roaring like fiends; so we experienced a storm at sea yet are safe. Monday morning finds us quite well, the storm abated, sun shining brightly, wind blowing briskly.

Sitting calmly on deck again, I am reminded that it has been said of foreign travel, "The stay-at-home knows not the restfulness that descends upon the spirit with that sense of the futility of worry which the weighing of anchor brings. To the well a sea voyage offers usually a curious and interesting experience—as the shores fade in the distance, so the busy life upon them also fades into unreality; sitting on deck at nine in the morning, watching the sunlight sparkle on the water, we can think of what is going on at home—all this a part of the past before the world was bounded for you by the straight walls of a ship. Under these conditions one must rest—a barrier impossible to cross rises between you and your anxieties; distracted from its old solicitudes, the brain repairs itself."

SUNDAY.—Religious services were held in dining-hall. About sixty were present; second-class passengers were among the worshippers; simple services, I am told. I was too sick to be present. About eight hundred souls on board, crew and all; a well-managed ship, seventy-five coal heavers, a printing office, barber-shop, reading-room with fine library for the benefit of passengers, a great variety of books; the ship is lighted with electric-lights, which are turned out at 11 o'clock P. M.

JUNE 11TH.—Yesterday passed like most days at sea, except for the expectation of seeing land at any time, and the seagulls flying about the ship—as they do, it is said, on approaching land. The day was charming as to weather, the sea calm as a lake; very many are preparing their mail to send off at Queenstown. I added thereto six letters and a cablegram sent to friends at home.

III.

"The Green Coast of Erin."

About five o'clock in the afternoon, English time, four and a half hours later than New York time, a slight white cloud was seen in the far distant horizon, hardly visible to the naked eye, said to be land —the rocky coast of Ireland, which gradually became more distinct. About seven P. M., on coming on deck after dinner, we were delighted to see land again. The coast was rocky, like the Palisades on the Hudson or the coast of Maine—almost perpendicular rocks, with the waves of the ocean dashing and breaking into white foam. The setting sun on the hilltop was a pleasing sight after watching it sink in the ocean for days and days; the hills were slightly green—a passenger suggested one would have to wear green glasses to see it. A Scotch lady who had crossed many times said they were not usually green. I saw with interest the light off "Fastnet," where the first intelligence of the sight of steamers is cabled to America—it is a lighthouse on a large rock far from shore, a desolate-looking place to live. We arrived at Queenstown at one o'clock at night, some passengers remaining up to see passengers disembark. A cablegram from home was received here telling us that all was well—joyful news! We have been steaming away the balance of the night, and shall continue to do so until three o'clock this afternoon, when we leave the ship and take a tender, so-called, to take us up the Mersey to Liverpool, fifteen miles. The distance from Liverpool to Queenstown is two hundred and twenty miles, Holyhead and coast of Wales to be seen en route. The steamer travels about eighteen knots an hour; average distance three hundred and ninety-one miles a day on this voyage, over four hundred miles some days. We reached Liverpool about six o'clock P. M. After some delay at custom-house, we were taken in a carriage to our hotel, the "Northwestern," at the terminus of railroad by that name, as good as any in Liverpool, so said. We enjoyed the drive there through the streets, the first sight of a foreign city, immensely. Everything looked odd; the street cars, drawn by three horses, one as a leader, carried as many passengers on top nearly as inside; a double row seated back to back, reading newspapers as they rode, as unconcerned as possible; winding stairs leading up from back platform. The omnibuses drove three horses abreast, all larger than American horses, the Norman breed. Much use is made of donkeys in drawing carts, and even to drive with loads of children ; we were amused at seeing many happy parties of them. A sad sight was four little children forming a street band, all respectably dressed—three girls, and a boy with a bass-viol as large as himself. Our bedrooms at our hotels are models of comfort ; large rooms, with wide, high beds ; linen sheets, spotlessly white, at least three yards wide ; brass bedsteads, with canopy of beautiful chintz, white ground, with pink rosebuds in pattern ; window curtains to match, with handsome border of heavy white cotton fringe that could be laundered ; rich mahogany wardrobe ; washstand, like a table, marble top, with tiling above on back, and a brass rod running from two upright posts, with white mull shirred upon it, giving a neat effect, the mahogany polished highly ; the " cabinet " had mahogany seats ; walls painted to imitate wainscoting in dark red—good effect.

After dinner we drove out to Princes Park and Sefton Park, leaving the hotel at half-past eight P. M., not dark ; a delightful drive, seeing many unique dwellings, the bricks looking smoky and of various colors ; some handsome houses, residences of the merchants of Liverpool, all back from

the street, with pretty yards in front, with flowers
and shrubbery. We are just in time to see the
rhododendrons in bloom; they are later than
usual, so we have the benefit of a late season.
The parks abound in them, of pale pink color,
deep pink ; the laburnum are in blossom, beautiful, too—a drooping yellow flower, very abundant, something like our wisteria in form ; trees
and shrubs of laburnum, covered with the rich
yellow blossoms ; the hawthorn trees, both white
and pink, are in bloom—nothing could be more
beautiful; the hedges, with which England
abounds, are just blossoming. Altogether, we
could not have come in a more desirable time. I
am charmed with the country ; the roads are excellent, macadamized, so hard and smooth.

IV.

Sight Seeing in England.

FRIDAY, JUNE 12.—We took a delightful drive this morning to Childwall Abbey, an old abbey, a sort of public restaurant, where we lunched at a quaint old house, covered with ivy. Saw some carved mahogany furniture of queer style, 300 years old; the paper on wall up-stairs was very old, and had representations of Mother Goose Melodies, Little Bo-peep, and all that was very funny; the garden attached was extensive; a long hedge of rhododendrons in bloom; large red peonies, pansies, very fine specimens, bordered many beds.

The drive to the Abbey was through a fine country, gentleman's estates, houses almost hidden by trees, high stone walls covered with a luxuriant growth of ivy; porters' lodges of quaint design, all looking very neat, and flowers everywhere, the ivy overhanging the walls and drooping to the roadside: beautiful meadows and fields highly cultivated, with fine, large cattle and sheep grazing in them—England is famous for excellent mutton

—no weeds by roadside anywhere. Two laborers we passed on the way, with their trousers tied just below the knee with wisps of grass, carried bunches of laburnum blossoms, yellow and pink hawthorn, which we were wishing for; they ran after the carriage and gave them to us; of couse, we reward them, with an English sixpence, which satisfied them. We were enjoying the day and the drive so much that it seemed as if everything we wanted came to us. A charming day—the "cabby" said it was the finest in three weeks; we were much pleased with Liverpool.

Opposite our hotel was St. George's Hall; in front of this building were two colossal lions, carved in stone, also equestrian statues of Victoria and Albert and the statue of Lord Beaconsfield (Disraeli), the latter in centre; the streets were well paved and very clean; miles of fine stone docks; much of interest everywhere, we thought. We left in afternoon train for Chester, an old walled city; enjoyed the ride of fifteen miles by rail through fine country; even the poorest houses are picturesque; arrived at about 5 P. M. To improve our time took carriage and drove for two hours about the town and visited the old cathedral, begun in the eleventh century, built of red sandstone, falling to decay, many places being renovated, and has been all along down the vista of years a great curiosity ; grand carvings, symbolic of Scripture events ; mosaic of the Lord's Supper ; very fine old gobelin tapestry hangs on wall ; also battle flags, taken at the battle of Bunker Hill, carried by a regiment of English soldiers ; a beautiful Bible and altar cloth inlaid with precious stones, amethyst, topaz, emeralds ; the book-mark in Bible decorated with fine pearls ; fine frescoes on ceiling ; old gothic church. We visited an old house, bearing date 1591, that an earl took refuge in when pursued ; was hidden six weeks up under the roof, and was at last found by spies.

Chester was one of the chief military stations of the Romans in Britian. It is the best possible entrance to the England of an American traveler's dreams—the England that he had so long desired to see and upon whose threshold he stands at last. If he wants to find himself really in a foreign land let him go to Chester.

The "Rows" are a curious feature of the two main streets, running through the city at right angles. Besides the ordinary sidewalk, there is a continuous covered gallery through the front of the second story of the houses. On this up-stairs street all the better class of shops are situated ;

the others underneath on a level with the roadway. As some one has said, great is the puzzle of the stranger as to whether the roadway is down in the cellar, or he is up-stairs on the landing, or the house has turned itself out at the window. We passed in driving a very old house of wood, with this inscription on the front, in large plain letters, " God's providence is mine inheritence," said to have escaped the plague in the sixteenth century, the only one, and is called God's providence house. We are stopping at the " Queen's " hotel—the Grosvener being the most popular but full, the Duke of Westminster holding a yearly drill, he being at head of the troops. We saw him enter the cathedral yesterday—a man of sixty and odd, with a young wife of twenty-six; he looked like an ordinary soldier, tall and erect. He has a magnificent estate, the finest in England; he is called, in fact, the richest man in the kingdom. This house or palace is thrown open to the public for a small fee, all the grounds and lower story; the money given to charity, men servants to escort visitors about and explain matters.

The second day of our stay in Chester, June 13, took a drive of three miles before reaching the entrance to the park or grounds of this fine estate; rode about three miles further before reaching the castle, through fine grounds; a fee of one shilling is required for admittance, when a guide or servant walks with you; no admittance till 11 A. M. The floor of long halls as you enter is of mosaic, in black and white half-inch squares; busts of white marble on pedestals and rare vases of pottery on either side of the hall; bust of Michael Angelo. Leading from this hall was another that led to the family chapel, now being renovated. A life-size marble statue of the Duke's first wife reclined at one side of the altar; beautiful stained glass window opposite the entrance. At further end of main hall were cabinets let in the wall, lined with colors to show the rare china; the ceiling was beautiful, in white and gold. Stained glass windows of rare beauty adorned this hall, some of which were open, for the day was warm and delightful, and revealed grounds beautifully laid out with flower-beds in various forms; artificial lakes, trees trained in forms and distant landscapes. We then enter state dining-room, very large, elegantly carved high mantels, an immense window opposite the mantel. At either end of the room hung life-sized portraits of the present Duke of Westminster, his first wife and his father and mother. Very fine floors, all of oak, to be used with rugs. The present Duke has eight children ; the portraits of them all—fine paintings—hang in the ante dining-room, a smaller one, countesses by the quantity, viscounts to match. The drawing-room was immense, with Gobelin tapestry covering the furniture, richest velvet brocade on some pieces ; the wood all gilt, ceiling all gilt and delicate colors. One room was painted and fitted up in Japanese style ; painted just above the wainscoting were birds, storks and cranes, some pink, some drab ; mantels of various colored marble, all very high. The library was also a music-room, a large organ in one end ; woodwork of this room was American oak ; mantel inlaid with mother of pearl ; a barometer in centre over mantel connected with weather-vane on top of the house ; furniture in this room dark wood, Gobelin tapestry coverings ; tables, large and small, everywhere ; rare screens, fine paintings in oil on them ; books on side walls ; the entire spaces and height filled with rare books of miscellany, history, encyclopedias, history of birds of Australia, etc. ; on an easel was a life-size portrait of the present duchess, a niece of Lord Cavendish, painted by Millais ; grand staircase was white marble, with niches filled with armor.

All the way up from front entrance, through the *porte cochere*, is a view in a straight line of a road a mile and three-quarters long; on the grounds are fine brick houses for horses and dogs, almost a separate house and lot for each horse.

After visiting this fine estate, we drove through this long vista into the grounds of the then Premier, Gladstone, adjacent, several miles distant to his castle, Hawarden. He married these estates, they told us, and has lived there for fifty years near his castle on the old ruins of the former castle, built in 1000—very picturesque walls fifteen feet thick in places, now ivy-covered. We ascended the winding stairs to the summit, which overlooks a great extent of country—eight counties—and is connected, or was in feudal times, with Eaton Hall by an underground passage five miles long. Before entering these grounds we lunched at a queer old house called "Maria Jones' Inn."

V.

In London Town.

From this place, after a most delightful time, we went to our hotel, and prepared to take train for London, only a few hours' ride. Left late in the afternoon, arriving after dark in the great city, June 14th; took rooms at the Continental Hotel—very Frenchy, all attendants speaking English in a broken way. In all English hotels women are employed as clerks, dressed usually in plain black silk, and having much to do with the patrons of the house.

Harriet and I, after breakfast, took a "hansom" and drove to Mr. Spurgeon's church; heard him preach. This, our first experience, cost me a twelve-dollar parasol, which I left in the hansom, and overpaid the driver, he taking advantage of the situation. Spurgeon preached from the text, James v. and 11th, a good, practical sermon, dwelling on God being very pitiful. He worked for results, not the means, in afflicting His children, as in Job's case. Spurgeon's voice was clear and strong; could be distinctly heard through a large, very plain church (will seat 7,000 people), filled with an immense audience—two galleries, the lower one with seven rows of seats; back of the pulpit nine rows; second gallery five rows; all well filled, with seats in aisles; congregational singing. We crossed Westminster bridge, one of London's fine bridges of stone across the river Thames; saw the Parliament buildings, near this bridge, on bank of the Thames—immense structures of stone; in fact, no wooden buildings are seen in England, either large or small—all of brick or stone.

Monday we visited Westminster Abbey for a short time; intend going again; also took a drive in Hyde Park, the fashionable drive; saw great numbers of fine equipages and very many equestrians; the carriages or their occupants were not so showy or stylish as in Central Park, New York, but very substantial; saw the Royal coach, a yellow-bodied, large carriage, drawn by four horses, preceded by a horseman, loaded with rich trappings, blowing a horn; all carriages drove to either side to allow it a broad space in centre, and stood still until it passed.

Next day visited the Cyrstal Palace, a wonderful structure of glass, filled with statuary, growing plants, ferns and palms; booths innumerable for the sale of small wares ; a band of music, playing fountains, also picture-gallery on second floor, stuffed animals in great variety ; about one hour's ride by rail on Northern Railway from Victoria Station, London, through the city and adjacent villages, Brixton and all sorts of English names, connecting with London ; fine parks on the way. England is a delightful country. We are agreeably surprised. The buildings in London are mostly three stories high, but broad, built of stone in a lasting manner. We drove to London Tower for a tour of inspection, but found visitors were denied admission since the late attempt to destroy the Tower with dynamite. We found this out to our regret. We visited the Zoological Gardens in Regent's Park—a wonderful collection of birds, beasts and reptiles, grounds well laid out with plants and flowers, fountains and good walks ; also took a short ride on Underground Railroad, and visited Madame Tussaud's waxworks, one of London's popular places of resort ; one room devoted to relics of Napoleon—his carriage in which he traveled, the bed on which he died, rings and various articles of presents he made to relatives and friends, cameo rings, watches, etc.

We left London, after a ten days' stay, at 3 P. M., for Dover, going through a charming country

—a three hours' ride by rail—passing quaint houses, windmills, fine meadows bordered with hedges, some hilly scenery, all so varied, so fresh and green, in this leafy month of June—just a little hazy. We were charmed.

As we approached Dover the channel burst upon our view; wind blowing quite strong, waves dashing. Harriet and I were quite disheartened, as we intended crossing it, and feel discouraged at the prospect of braving its dangers and going to a far country on the Continent, where a strange language is spoken. In the morning we walked out to the end of a long stone pier, and saw a steamer leave for Calais, France. Can hardly realize that we are so near continental Europe. This immensely long and strong pier, built of solid masonry, was thirty years building. Steamers from Ostend, Belgium, start from this pier—four hours' ride across the channel—and from Calais, France, land here. The shortest passage is 21 miles, consuming one and one-half hours. Have visited Dover Castle and Tower, the former said to have been built by the Normans, before Christ, in their invasion of England; built of lava, brought as ballast, certainly very ancient, and a strong fortress situated on a high hill, overlooking the channel, still occupied by a garrison (the

Castle) ; plenty of red-coated soldiers on duty now, 320 feet above the level of the sea. We are stopping at the Lord Warden Hotel (very English), near the pier and railroad; a fine hotel. Fifty thousand inhabitants in Dover.

VI.

On the Continent.

We crossed the English Channel, twenty-one miles to Calais, an old French town of which we saw but little save the queer old houses, the peculiar dress of the women and children; the jabbering of French language, too, sounded odd, having heard nothing but English spoken two hours before. We took train for Paris. The cars were luxuriously fitted up with light gray cloth upholstery, with dark blue silk curtains, heavy cords and tassels in fine taste. We enjoyed the ride through pleasant country and small towns, stopped at Amiens, where James bought a paper of lunch and a bottle of claret, which we disposed of at our leisure and enjoyed too. People approached the cars with long baskets, fitted up in a tasty, tempting manner, with bread and fruits, arranged with green leaves (grape leaves) and bottles of wine, so unlike American venders. There was an interpreter on the train, though we had no occasion to employ him. The seats in all cars in Europe are facing each other, divided in compartments, windows and doors on the sides, each compartment designed to hold eight. We were alone. Our party so rode all day through "La Belle France," reaching Paris about six in the afternoon ; got through the Custom-house quickly by feeing an officer to the small sum of 2 francs ; got in cab with all our bags and baggage on top of same and inside, so with no further trouble drove to the "Continental Hotel," same name as in London, though a much larger, finer hotel, magnificiently furnished ; large dining-rooms and reading-room, tables in same, with paper pens and ink, all conveniences for writing ; all the papers of the day of different countries supplied. The hotel is built with an open court, has a piazza or promenade all around ; carriages all drive into this court, and all arrive or depart from it. The promenade has a mosaic floor ; all attendants speak both French and English ; the hotel is " beautiful for situation," as well as in itself, being opposite the garden of the Tuileries, the garden being kept at public expense and thrown open, with its beautiful avenues, statuary, fountains, trees and flowers—a pleasure to be near and behold, in a warm June day especially.

JUNE 24TH.—Have driven and walked much and crossed the river Seine, the city being built on both sides of the river, connected by fine stone bridges, long rows of trees on either side of river, houses peering above the trees and back of them. The boats used on the river are about the size of our canal boats and used for excursions and pleasure.

Have been to the "Bon Marche," a store of immense size, with merchandise in great variety and at prices that tempt female tourists. A fine drive of fifteen minutes from our hotel, in going, passed the Louvre; have not yet visited it, with its vast art treasures; also passed all that remains of the Tuileries destroyed in 1871, and not rebuilt. Have seen the Column Vendome that was also destroyed, but rebuilt from same castings, they having been found—designs all over it commemorating battles. Took a drive in the Bois de Boulogne at the fashionable hour; saw immense numbers of carriages and great style in dress; it is a beautiful park, with fine roads, shaded walks and trees. It is four miles square, and has seventy acres of lakes or artificial water. The "Champs Elysees" is at the entrance of the avenue that leads to the "Bois." Its wide avenue, seats and places of refreshment make it a gay resort in the evening, and pleasant to walk or drive in at any time. Have been to see the world-renowned church of "Notre Dame," a magnificent building, with its carvings, statuary and immense stained-glass windows. The greater part of this church is said to have been built in the thirteenth century, but was renovated and restored since 1845; it escaped injury during the late war and under the Commune; also saw the exterior of the church "Madeline," with its Corinthian columns and carvings over front entrance.

JUNE 25TH.—Visited the Louvre to-day, an immense structure, a palace noted for its magnificence and its art treasures of paintings by the old masters; the original Murillo of the Madonna is here, elegant Gobelin tapestries of the fourteenth and fifteenth centuries, life-likenesses of kings in Gobelin adorned the walls; the ceilings of immense height, frescoed with rare paintings, and case after case of rare old china and crystal in odd designs, very fine. The palace was begun in 1528 by Francis I., and added to by succeeding kings, until Louis XIV., and finished by Napoleon I. in 1803. It is well known that Charles IX. occupied this palace, Henry III. and Henry IV., and Louis XIII. and Louis XV. during part of his minority. Since that it has been devoted to its present purpose; gardens with flowers are kept in order all around the palace; the latter runs parallel with the river

Seine, overlooks the river from some of the second-story balconies. I could form no estimate of the length of this palace ; should judge it was at least two squares or city blocks ; trees are all along the river side ; in fact Paris is full of trees, streets with double lines of them, and all along the banks of the river. Have seen the Arc de Triomphe, erected by Napoleon I. in 1806, to commemorate his battles and victories ; it is built of gray marble, with one central arch and two side arches, smaller on top. In centre is a large piece of sculpture—a female—representing Victory, in a triumphal car, and four bronzed horses attached, a magnificent work; one sees it in going to the Bois de Boulogne ; it is surrounded by stone posts and chains for protection. The Column Vendome I have also seen, it being not far from the Hotel Continental, where we are stopping, the hotel—almost a palace itself, facing the garden of the Tuileries, with its avenues, trees, fountains, flowers and statuary. The street on which this hotel is situated is the Rue de Rivoli ; it is on a corner ; the other street is Rue de Castiglioni.

The Column Vendome stands in a large open square, where many of the best residences are. It is 135 feet high, is covered with bas-reliefs commemorating scenes from the past history of the glory of France, was pulled down by the Communists in 1871, but as I have said, models being found, was again rebuilt. The palace of the Tuileries was also destroyed at this time, and has not been rebuilt. The pavilions or entrances thereto are still standing.

JUNE 28TH.—This day visited the Gobelin tapestry manufactories sustained by government —established in 1662; saw wonderful copies of fine paintings in colors so fine and smooth, many pieces taking years to execute—five years—many colored worsteds on bobbins like weavers; there would be thirty shades of one color. Many of these tapestries were as old as the fifteenth century, and were dropping to pieces. None are sold to the public —only for royalty. Also rode eight miles on the river Seine in one of the small steamers that are running constantly for passengers—passed under at least a dozen fine bridges, mostly stone and arched, with sculpture ornamenting them of various designs—to visit the Sévres porcelain works, pronounced "Sev." I bought a small vase as a memento of our visit; saw beautiful vases at fabulous prices, from a thousand dollars up, of all colors and designs; was not so pleased as with the exhibition of Gobelin tapestries, though; saw the clay, the models, and china in different stages of manufacture, also the kilns or ovens for burning or baking it ; returned to a late dinner at our hotel, which was highly relished, having been out since morning sight-seeing.

VII.

AT VERSAILLES.

JUNE 29TH.—Took a carriage and had a delightful drive to Versailles, about fourteen miles distant from Paris, and nearly connected to it by suburban towns, picturesque too; passed some markets—it being morning—that were unlike home in display of wares, flowers and vegetables; each kind and color of flower anywhere for sale in Paris is in a bunch by itself, put up with plain white paper, enhancing the color by contrast, and being attractive; long lines of trees of double rows— sometimes five rows—all trimmed, much same size, forming beautiful avenues for walking or driving; we drove along the river Seine for some distance, on a high embankment, and a wall of solid masonry on side next river; could see the boats plying.

The day was fine, neither too warm nor too cold, and we enjoyed the drive immensely, arriving duly at Versailles, formerly a large city of 100,000, now a town of half that size. In the reign of Louis XIV. and Louis XV., the royal family, court and officers resided here. We first visited on our entrance to the palace grounds what is called the Great Trianon. This and the Little Trianon, or *petite* as it is called in French, are both in the great park, some distance from the palace, in comparison with which they seem insignificant. The Great Trianon is exquisitely furnished; was occupied by Napoleon I and Josephine; her sleeping-room and bed are still the same, with canopy of silken curtains and furniture, the chairs mostly white wood. In some rooms the walls are upholstered in silk damask. Many of them have been reproduced in imitation or duplicate of former stuff. Napoleon seemed to prefer yellow for coloring, his rooms being furnished with a bright canary yellow; the clocks, vases, pictures, tables, all very rich, writing desks, dressing tables and cabinets inlaid and beautiful, the floors mostly hard wood, marble mantels of various colors, with wide fire-places and low andirons. The Palace is but one story high; a great number of rooms on one floor. Did not visit the Little Trianon : said to be no furniture there and little of interest; built by Louis XIV. for Marie Antionette. Saw her rooms also in the great palace, a very small mirror with angles in this room in which she saw herself headless, so had a presentiment of coming doom. I looked myself in this mirror and saw the same effect. Not far from Great Trianon is the building containing carriages—a great display of historical sleighs and carriages of great interest. Saw Josephine's carriage, the coronation carriage and the one Empress Eugénie rode in, lined with white satin and richly gilded and decorated, of very large size, to be drawn by eight horses. Saw sedan chairs used by Marie Antoinette and other royal personages. After this we drove to Versailles, or out of the park, and lunched; returning visited the great palace built by Louis XIV., improved and added to by his successors.

The Great Trianon was a favorite residence of Louis XIV., Louis XV. and Louis XVI., also Napoleon I.; the latter built a road from it to St. Cloud, not far distant—St. Cloud, destroyed during the siege of 1871 and not rebuilt, celebrated for its fine parks even now. The grand palace was once a hunter's lodge; in 1624 used by Henry IV., and Louis XIII. In 1660 Louis XIV., becoming tired of his other palaces, undertook building this; it was added to by succeeding kings at great expense; Louis Phillip restored it last, converting it into a vast museum, rich and splendid. It contains immense pictures of battle scenes commemorating the history of France. One hall or gallery is 327 feet long, filled with marble busts; another room contains portraits of seventy-one kings, down to Louis Phillip; five large rooms devoted to paintings of the Crusade, the ceilings and walls are covered with armorial emblems of French knights who fought in the Holy Land. The palace is very large, built of stone, with two immense wings; we saw the room and bed where Louis XIV. died; the bed is on a raised platform, this covered with red velvet, the bedstead all gilt, with very high canopy curtains of silk falling at sides, now discolored with age; bed covering of same over the pillows with Honiton lace spread at foot of bed; some pictures and inlaid furniture on either side of bed, and a railing of gilt with a gate separates this from the rest of the room. This room was in centre of the palace; in second story a balcony in front of a large window, with a clock above, now running, but formerly only told the hour one king died and his successor was announced. The death of the king was proclaimed from this balcony; it overlooks the beautiful park, with its world renowned fountains of immense size, that were playing the day we visited this grand historical place; the water was brought a great distance to supply these fountains. When the grounds were being made the gardens and parks thirty thousand soldiers, 'tis said, worked upon them simultaneously; even now, 1885, the flower beds are in perfect order, flowers abundant, statuary of every kind, beautiful trees trimmed in various forms, and not a depredation committed ; all open to the public at certain hours ; a sight of all these fine historical paintings granted free. One large painting that interested me was the coronation of the Empress Josephine by Napoleon in the Church of *Notre Dame*, very beautiful in color and execution. I was never more forcibly reminded, in viewing all this magnificence, that "the glory of this world passeth away." It seemed as if each succeeding king or emperor tried to outdo his predecessor in grandeur and use of money. One wonders, in coming from democratic America, where all the money came from ; but then we are apt to forget that this country is centuries old and has been enriched by preying on other countries. Eastern countries of great wealth have been despoiled to add to the glory and art treasures of France. One immense hall in this large palace or gallery, as it is called, is the " Grand Gallery of Glass ; " the central building measuring 239 feet long, 35 feet wide, 43 feet high, lighted by seventeen large arched windows, which correspond with arches on opposite wall of Venetian mirrors, time of Louis XIV. Mirrors were not then made of present size, so these are in smaller divisions.

Sixty Corinthian pillars of red marble, with base and capitals of gilt bronze, fill the intervals between the windows. Each of the entrances is adorned with columns of same order. The arched ceiling was painted by Lebrun in nine large and eighteen smaller compartments, representing principal events in the history of Louis XIV. in allegory. A beautiful chapel is also attached to this palace, with stained-glass windows and much gilding, paintings, etc. The fountains in the park of immense size need to be seen to be appreciated. Long lines of shaded walks with statuary that look ancient are in every direction. A marvelous place, indeed! I can picture with my pen but a faint idea of it.

Rooms almost without number, filled with paintings, that I have not mentioned.

We visited the Palace of Luxembourg this afternoon. It has been in time palace, prison, senate chamber; it is now devoted to art, paintings and sculpture; fine flower gardens surround it; palace built in time of Henry I. and Henry II. Also went to the Garden of Plants in old part of Paris, used now as a place of resort and park by the poorer classes; fine old trees, but the garden not attractive nowadays.

VIII.

SWITZERLAND THE MAGNIFICENT.

JULY 2D.—To-day we left the beautiful city of Paris after a ten or twelve days' visit, taking a train for Geneva, Switzerland, a long ride of 391 miles by rail, passed through many old French towns ; saw peasant women working in fields and gardens same as men, a hardy-looking race. As we approached Geneva we saw high ranges of mountains (the Alps) vine-clad ; every available spot had a patch of grapes up the steep mountain sides, and small low huts here and there occupied by the peasants who cultivated and protected the growing grapes, making a very picturesque scene, which evinced great industry and frugality. We also rode through many tunnels, I should judge at least a dozen of various lengths, one of them taking the train twenty-five minutes to pass through. It seemed fearfully dark and dangerous ; as we approached Geneva the wildest scenery greeted our eyes. A river emerged, a wild stream in a deep ravine, which proved to be the river Rhone ; it flows from Lake Geneva and divides that city into two parts, which are connected by six bridges. We arrived in Geneva at half-past nine o'clock in the evening, and it was dark when we were driven to our hotel—Hotel La Paix by name. It is beautifully situated, we discovered ; when morning dawned on Lake Geneva, with snow-caped Alps towering in sight on opposite shore of the lake, I could hardly believe my eyes. A beautiful scene— steamboats arriving and departing just in sight of our windows, the lake a calm sheet of water as our Mohawk river, and not as wide here as I supposed. One forms such different ideas of places and things from what seeing or the reality discloses. A beautiful park across the street from our hotel contains a very high and elegant monument, erected to the memory of the Duke of Brunswick, who gave large sums of money to the City of Geneva. It is an equestrian statue ; on the very top a stone cap just large enough for the horse and rider to stand on—a great work of art to balance such an object on so small a space and at such height.

We took a carriage and drove about the city to the Botanical Garden and about the streets, which were narrow in many places; drove up a hill where we had a view of the two rivers flowing side by side, the Rhone and the Arve

—one of deep blue and clear, the other muddy, coming down from the mountains.

Though a large city, we did not find Geneva so interesting as many others we have visited. We remained only two nights and a day, left early on the morning of July 4th, sent a cablegram to my husband in America, saying, "Glorious day, all well," which I hope was duly received. We were to take seats in diligence from Geneva to Chamouni in the Alps, a ride of fifty miles, but could not get desirable seats, not having engaged them soon enough, having decided to leave a day sooner than we at first intended; so took a carriage, which was far more comfortable and commodious, also more expensive; so with traveling-bags, bundles, shawl straps, etc., etc., we started for a long ride. It rained for a couple of hours, then cleared; the sun came out very hot; we had a small traveling thermometer, which indicated 86 degrees part of the time, though icy and snow-capped mountains were in sight. The ride was a gradual ascent all the way to Chamouni; most excellent roads macadamized and very fine—in fact, we have found such everywhere in Europe, so far. In England, France and Switzerland, such a contrast to the neglected roads in our native land! We passed through interesting old French villages; everywhere neatness and industry were evident; land well cultivated. An appearance of poverty with contentment seemed to prevail.

About half past twelve we alighted for luncheon at a place called Salon, an old town. In fact, one sees little that is new or enterprising like our young America. We were treated to little trout caught in the mountain stream, that were well cooked and very sweet and palatable, after our ride of several hours. We saw peddlers of cheap crockery and glass; their wares spread upon the ground. After resting we started up and on our way, still climbing the mountain road, high peaks in sight in every direction, with snow and ice glistening in the sun, yet the valley was warm, even hot. Where there were steep precipices or dangerous places excellent masoned stone walls were built for protection, giving travelers a sense of relief.

This long day's ride of fifty miles takes three relays of horses to accomplish, the diligence having five horses, three in front as leaders and two behind; others six horses, three abreast. Three diligences started from Geneva this day, beside other conveyances. The scenery was novel and grand. Before reaching Chamouni we passed glaciers upon the sides of the mountains with fields of blue ice standing up in sharp points like towers or turrets, the glaciers extending down nearly to the road we were traveling. The horses of our carriage, as well as those attached to the diligence, all had small bells, like old-fashioned sleigh-bells, on their necks, the tinkling sound thereof not unmusical, but being odd enough to modern travelers. We reached Chamouni before nightfall, stopping at a hotel called L'Angletaire ; we found the host and waiters spoke fairly good English. We had delightful rooms adjoining, furnished with taste and comfort. On the mantel was a clock, with side ornaments to match. A maid brought warm water to our rooms, immediately on our arrival, in pewter pitchers. From my window, it seemed but a stone's throw, was the foot of the great Mont Blanc, with snow several feet deep, that seemed to extend to nearly the foot of it, this July day—a wonderfully grand sight that I never shall forget. Mont Blanc is sixteen thousand feet high. The town lies in a small valley surrounded by mountains, but Mont Blanc soars above them all. The view of the sun rising upon this mountain, which I had the pleasure of seeing, was grand beyond my power of description, a river pouring down from the mountain ran rapidly in sight of the hotel. The American flag was displayed in honor of our natal day, July 4th, and fireworks also, out of compliment to Americans. Three men were ascending the mountain, were half-way up it, taking two days to make the ascent, each with a guide. At night they took shelter in a small hut, and displayed a red light that all could see from the hotel and village—a dangerous trip.

We were told that ladies rarely undertook the ascent. We remained over night only at this very comfortable inn, walked out in the early evening, the streets being very narrow and odd; saw peasant women driving cows through the streets, the cows having small tinkling bells on their necks. The cows graze upon the mountain sides, are watched through the day, and driven from door to door and milked according to the quantity each family requires. All seemed to live out of doors, the women knitting and seemingly happy. All walked in the middle of the streets, as the walks were only about two feet wide. We left, with regret, this unusual town.

At nine o'clock in the morning took two small carriages to go to Martigny, James and the courier engaged in Paris in one, Harriet and I in the other, two-seated, small-wheeled vehicles, with two horses (with bells), and a driver for each—little knowing what was in store for us. It began to rain soon after starting our wagons—they could not be called carriages they were so uncomfortable and hard—riding a distance of sixty miles, from Chamouni to Martigny, over mountains; we were started on a perilous ride. At first we drove over a level road for some distance. The courier said the drive would be through wilder scenery than the day before.

Nothing daunted, we started, having had a pleasant drive the day before through wonderful scenery. We did not expect the experiences of the second day. We began to climb mountains where the roads were poor and stony, in many places so narrow we could not have passed another vehicle; over old, rickety bridges and wild streams, each hour becoming more wild and grand, till we reached the climax of mountain travel, and winding around black, rocky mountains that were the more dangerous-looking from the falling rain, each turn seeming to be the end of the road that was hardly wider than the vehicle we were in; high rocks and mountains on one side and a yawning abyss on the other, with a roaring river running furiously at the bottom, down, down so deep and dangerous, mortal eyes dared not gaze on a scene so dreadful. I would never have dreamed that I could be brought to ride in such a situation. On and on we went, no alternative but this. It filled me with such terror as I hope never to again experience, and should not have undertaken had I known what was before me ; in fact, must confess ignorance of this dangerous pass " Tete Noire," till brought to my knowledge by sad experience. The driver could not speak English, so that my entreaties for him to stop and let me try and walk were in vain. We were provided with Alpine stocks as most persons are who walk around this most dangerous point, but the rain and mud prevented. Harriet thought it would be impossible for us to walk ; there was no fine stone wall for protection on this dangerous road, nothing apparently between us and certain death in this awful manner but the direct interpositon of a kind Providence. I cried like a child, fear overcoming every sense ; *could not* see the grandeur or beauty of scenery that many would have enjoyed, from o'ermastering fear. Even now I shudder in writing of it ; the driver whipped up his horses, cracking his whip with all complacency, both horses and driver quite accustomed to the route, it being daily traveled.

I could not sleep at night after this adventure, even when snugly housed in a comfortable room and bed, my nerves had been so shocked—could not banish the sight of the mountains and precipices and horrible scenery.

After passing this point we rode through a tunnel. Emerging from this we came to a hotel not far off, built on a point of projecting rocks, called the "Tete Noire" house, where we rested for an hour and a half, dined with many others who were traveling over the same route we had just passed. Then we proceeded over dangerous (to me) mountain roads, still ascending, afterward descending, the road turning with a sharp curve and winding round and round on the descent, scarcely any protection on the narrow, winding way ; having had so recent a shock in going over the "Tete Noire" that all seemed fraught with danger.

We were all the afternoon winding around and descending until at last the valley was reached and I breathed freely ; the sights and experiences of this day will never be forgotten. We arrived at Martigny at five o'clock after this eventful ride. From Martigny tourists go to the St. Bernard and other places in the Alps. Little of note in the village ; from here we took train for a short ride, bringing us out of this mountainous country to a place called Vevay, three hours' ride. Remained all night at a delightful hotel, with fine grounds leading to the Lake of Geneva, the other extremity from City of Geneva, with flowers abundant in the grounds of same varieties that we have at home—scarlet, pink and white geraniums, hollyhocks, etc.—flowers that seem to be common in every country—trees and shrubs ; birds sang most sweetly ; I think they were mocking birds ; a band of music played for an hour or two on piazza in the morning ; a most enjoyable spot to linger in.

We left at 12 o'clock, taking cars for a short ride 1½ hours to Berne, a quaint old town, with shops in arcades, a few feet above the street, buildings of stone, sewers in middle of the street, and women washing at pumps or places provided in street. We drove to the den of bears, brown bears, for which the place is famous ; bears are the emblem or crest of the place. We were here only a few hours, Harriet buying some ancient pewter jugs of curious workmanship that pleased her greatly. From here went by rail to Thun, a couple of hours' ride, then took boat, the cars stopping at boat-landing. Then we crossed Lake Thun, quite a wide, long lake, too nearly dark to enjoy the scenery, which was fine. Landed at or quite near Interlaken, fifteen minutes' ride from boat, a fine town filled with hotels. We are stopping at the "Victoria," the grounds of which are beautifully laid out, electric lights, fountains playing and everything quite palatial; in sight is the snow-covered mountain called the "Young Frau," with the rising and setting sun; the reflection and view are wonderfully fine. The village is small, 2,000 inhabitants, but said to be as many as 20,000 tourists here during the season. The birds sing more sweetly than any I ever heard; a musical locality; said to be no other birds in Switzerland; these in Interlaken came and every means are employed to propagate and keep them.

We have seen numbers of the peasants in their national dress. I saw about a dozen in this costume—women, walking with the men in procession, had just returned from a fair at Thun; each bore a vase with flowers, one in the middle a silver standard; this had been won at some contest; they walked six abreast with flags and a brass band—a novel sight. Plenty of shops in Interlaken for the sale of carved goods, wood in every variety, embroideries, photographs, etc., etc. We enjoyed our stay here exceedingly, found English spoken quite generally in the hotel and in the stores. Wild poppies grow here as daisies do with us, abound in fields and along railways; flowers are cultivated extensively everywhere in Europe; the humblest peasants have flowers in a garden if ever so small.

We left Interlaken at 9 A. M., the hotel host presenting every departing lady with a pretty bouquet of sweet-scented flowers. We had engaged for the day a comfortable, unique sort of double carriage that had accommodation for six persons; beside the driver, there were four of us with the courier. The ride was over mountain roads, the celebrated "Brunig Pass," 3,379 feet high, being on this route. The road was at a great height, but broad and firmly macadamized; the descent was quickly accomplished, the day bright and beautiful, the scenery ditto. Lake Brienz lay at our feet; snow-capped mountains in view on opposite shore of the lake, but how gladly we welcomed the valley road after this, to me, hazardous ride over mountain passes. The drive is forty-five miles in distance from Interlaken to Lucerne; passengers by diligence that runs daily go part way by boat on Lake Lucerne. We came all the way in carriage, arriving at seven o'clock in the evening, having dined at the hotel called the "Golden Lion" on the way.

Odd names are used for hotels in Europe; for instance, in the old town of Chester, England, names like these were seen: "Green

Dragon," " Old Nags Head," etc., certainly not enticing names to beguile strangers and pilgrims to. The hotel we were entertained in Lucerne is called Grand Hotel National; it is beautifully located on the banks of Lake Lucerne, only separated from the lake by wide walks, with seats under double rows of trees, trimmed in such form that an arch is the result, an arbor for shade, from which can be seen constantly passing steamboats and small boats ; the latter have canopies of striped yellow, while the boats and paddles are red, with bright red curtains, making things very showy and picturesque. On opposite side of the lake, the snowy Alps ranges are yet in sight—the " Rigi " being only four hours' ride from here, the ascent of which is by rail, an inclined plane 5,905 feet high.

JULY 10TH.—This morning we walked to see the famous Lion of Lucerne, which is a sight well worth a walk or a journey to see. A steep mountain is quite near the main street where a large and perfect lion is cut in the solid rock of the mountain side, the rock projecting over it like a canopy or cover. The lion is lying down. It was carved in memory of the Swiss Guards who lost their lives in defending the Tuileries" in 1792. This was once a French town ; the sculptor was Thorwaldsen.

We saw an old state house here in Lucerne, built in 1380; curious historical paintings on outside nearly defaced by the ravages of time; a large clock in tower of same building. The hour-hand represents the wild flower of the Alps, star-shaped. This clock struck the hour of 12 while we were gazing at it. Several very old drinking fountains of stone are in the streets bearing date of 1600; carved lion's heads, water spouting from their mouths, well worn by age.

We are resting here for a couple of days; have been engaged briskly writing letters home in the intervals of sight-seeing, in part to drive away home sickness. A concert was given by Tyrolese in costume in the hotel last evening; quite a novelty to us. Several old bridges are here, one of which Longfellow has made famous in his "Golden Legend." The bridge has paintings representing the history of Switzerland from an early date. Bridge built in 1600; paintings are in the gables, of the covering of the bridge on both sides of the gables, so that crossing in either direction one sees them, colors still undimmed; there are seventy of them. I bought a photograph of one picture to better impress my mind with them.

Harriet and I strolled out one afternoon to

attend an organ concert in a church 250 years old, filled with paintings of that age ; some portraits. The stone pavement was worn with use and age. The organ was fine, both sweet-toned and powerful, and well played. We paid one franc each for entrance fee.

IX.

Strasburg, The Rhine, Cologne.

We left this both old and new town this day, July 11th, at half-past one P. M., by train for Strasburg ; weather very hot ; rode through a rich farming country and wine-growing—that lost by France in the war of 1870. Arrived at 8.30 P. M., tired and dusty ; drove to hotel "Angleterre," took our tea in our room and enjoyed it much. Retired early. The next day, Sunday, we took a carriage to visit the old cathedral, where the world-renowned astronomical clock is—a wonder of art and sculpture—the cathedral being filled outside and in with carved figures, and having been built on foundation of a church in 1015, and this on site of one built in 510; was over 200 years in building. The façade was begun by Erwin Van Steinback and his daughter Sabina, to whom much of the fine sculpture is attributed ; was begun in 1277 and completed by John Hultz of Cologne in 1439. So history proves there have been notable women down the line of ages, and how year after year was consumed in constructing these wonderful cathedrals, of which nearly all the large cities in Europe can boast.

It has been said that the workmen or sculptors of these generations had rude instruments, very little help, and that they worked like God (with all reverence), so varied in expression is every face and form, the workmanship so perfect. This cathedral has been injured many times by lightning and earthquakes and war, the roof having been burnt by the German forces in the war of 1870, and as often rebuilt and kept in repair. A fund is in the hands of city authorities for this purpose. Bequests often have been left, the people having great pride in it, as well they may. I could have spent a longer time enjoyably than it was possible for me to do, admiring this wonderful structure.

A canal is in front of our Strasburg hotel; very narrow streets; plenty of soldiers everywhere. We passed the fortifications near the suburbs in driving two miles out, crossing a long pontoon bridge to have a look at the river Rhine for the first time; sun hot, and an uncomfortable drive. The streets are very narrow and little of interest except the cathedral and clock. Harriet, in a morning ramble, found quaint stores and made some purchases.

The Strasburg Astronomical Clock is beyond description—the most wonderful work of mechanism in the world. It winds itself 31st of December every year, and regulates itself by weights, never gets out of order, tells of the changes of the moon and all eclipses and planets, day of the month, hour of the day. At 12 o'clock each day a cock stationed on top of a pinnacle, perfect in resemblance to this bird, flaps its wings, throws back its head and crows three times, a little interval between. At same time there is the procession of the Apostles moving in front of the form of the Saviour, he raising his hand to bless them. Of the twelve apostles, Peter is the last. Each figure turns partly round and they bow as they pass; the figure of Death with a hammer in his hand strikes the hour; the figure of Childhood strikes the first quarter, Youth the second, Manhood the third, Old Age last. Beneath these figures are sun-chariots and figures representing the planets Jupiter, Mars, etc., one for each day of the week slowly moving, each day a new one. It was at 12 o'clock we were there, and the chariot representing Sunday was in full view. This clock was built to replace one made in the fourteenth century, called the Clock of the Three Sages. The clock ceased running for 200 years it was said. A new one was built in 1547 by order of the magistrate of the town in the place the present clock stands; it was not completed till 1574; it ceased running in 1789. In 1836 it was again repaired and set in motion, requiring over four years' time. Strasburg was the ancient capital of Alsace, in possession of France till 1871, now restored to Germany.

We left Strasburg at midday by train for Frankfort-on-the-Main. This river is navigable for small steamers, and in places is a rapid stream. Many bridges over it. In this city 140,000 inhabitants, a lively business town with fine open squares and many monuments or statues in them, a fine bronze one of Goethe and one of Schiller standing, of life-size or more. Saw the house where the former was born, now visited by tourists with interest; saw the oldest house in the city, the front of which is covered with paintings in bright colors of landscapes, portraits, life-size figures, making an odd appearance, date 1600. Also visited a museum where there was a beautiful piece of sculpture, in pure Italian marble, called "Adrienne;" was six years in being made by Danencker; rare work. Passed miles and miles of dense forests in going to and from Frankfort; we were not far from the famous Black Forest, and only thirty-eight miles from Baden Baden. While in Frankfort visted the Palm Garden a beautiful place with fountains, the perfection of carpet gardening, large trees, fine walks and music. The large palms were in a greenhouse arranged with great taste, a waterfall and grotto in centre, and among the palms the boxes containing palms were covered with bark and growing moss over them. People were seated about this garden, the ladies with work; many partaking of refreshments at small tables listening to the music, inhaling sweet odors of flowers; children with their maids romping about—a gay and attractive scene altogether, and one to be remembered as typical of Germany. Streets are very narrow in most of the city; old and odd houses everywhere.

We left this city early on the morning of July 15, took train for a couple of hours' ride, then embarked on a trim steamboat on the river Rhine. For the most of the day traveled on this world-renowed river, made so by poet and legend; passed the town of Bingen, also many ruins; castles on the highest points of ground having been used as fortresses in former times by lords and nobles who preyed on surrounding countries, and found refuge in these strongholds. They made the stream picturesque and unlike the rivers in our new country. The water was muddy however, and the river not so broad as I imagined.

Seeing is knowing. We passed a town called Johannisburg where the famous wine of that name is made. A bottle was procured and the party decided that it was superior. Among other notable towns we came to Coblentz, the summer residence of Kaiser Wilhelm, the old Emperor, who had recently arrived. Flags were flying from every available place, giving it a gay appearance in his honor. The place is strongly fortified.

On opposite shore is what is called the Gibraltar of the Rhine; thousands of troops are there stationed; farther on, we came to Bonn, an old university town; could only see the narrow streets leading from the river, and that it was much like all old German cities and twenty-one miles from Cologne, which city we reached at six o'clock in the afternoon, well tired with our steamer ride on the river Rhine. The day was fine, the steamer was overcrowded with passengers, so that we were confined mostly to our seats, which were uncomfortable. When the tall spires of the famous cathedral were visible, though many miles distant, we were glad—a curve in the river made the distance greater than it looked to be.

The morning after our arrival we took a carriage and drove to the cathedral, an immense structure, with spires 525 feet high and beautifully proportioned : considered the grandest gothic church in the world. It was begun in the twelfth century, work being done there now; the cathedral, like all these old ones, being constantly repaired and improved ; new figures made from the old designs. The stained-glass windows are marvels of richness and beauty of coloring, size and height. Immense sums of money have been lavished upon this church by kings, emperors and noblemen, and it is justly the pride of Germany. The location is not good. Too large a building for the space it occupies, old buildings and narrow streets crowding it—streets, many of them very narrow, the one upon which is the hotel " Disch," which we are sojourning at, is so narrow we can almost reach across it. Gloomy and dirty. In the modern part of the city that is fast being built the houses are fine and streets broad ; buildings four and five stories high ; we saw a fine statue of Frederick William III. in the market place, an equestrian on top surrounded by his generals, life-size, standing on every side in bronze—very natural ; also a statue of Bismarck in a small park ; Von Moltke in another park.

Cologne was once a walled city, and gates or entrances with towers are yet to be seen; the market in an open square was quite a novel sight ;

women, old and young, with white starched handkerchiefs tied over their heads instead of hats to protect them from the summer's sun, many bearing large baskets on their heads, using small round pads or cushions as a means of saving their brains from concussion, I suppose. All kinds of fruit and vegetables were displayed in baskets on the ground ; no tables or benches or any semblance of comfort to be seen. Both buyers and sellers seemed to be mostly women. We visited the Church of St. Ursula, very old, built in twelfth century, named after a noble woman ; said to have set out from Britain on a pilgrimage, with eleven thousand virgins as companions ; coming down the Rhine she landed at Cologne. St. Ursula had been a leader and a model of virtue and religion. They all fell into the hands of barbarians ; rather than submit to ignominious dishonor, her companions followed her example of courage and fortitude, preferring death to slavery and dishonor. She encouraged them to the last (so the story goes), calling to mind the heavenly reward they would receive hereafter. St. Ursula was pierced by the arrows of the Huns, many were killed by clubs and swords, all perished on the battlefield. The day of their death, October 21, is still celebrated as an anniversary. The church which stands over their tombs was formerly called the Church of the Holy Virgins; the foundation of the church was laid in the year 1000; the bones of these virgins were gathered up and are laid in every form in the walls of the church, said to be eight feet wide; I hardly know how deep with bones. The skulls are ranged in rows higher up, with glass before them, many with silver covering on them—a hideous idea. All this is shown visitors for a fee; a priest with long, black robes, rather rusty too, cadaverous-looking himself, recounts this story. St. Ursula is sculptured in alabaster, lying on her tomb with a dove at her foot; a bone of her arm is shown in the treasury. In a case is a thorn said to be from the Saviour's crown; other marvelous things are exhibited in this golden treasury, kept locked, only opened by an extra fee; many relics, very old—a water-pot said to be used at the wedding in Cana of Gallilee; an alabaster box looking very ancient, brought in the fourteenth century to Cologne by a knight from the Holy Land and presented to the city.

X.

THROUGH BELGIUM.

BRUSSELS, JULY 17TH.—We came from Cologne to this city this day on an express train that ran at a fearful rate of speed, making few stops. America is far in advance of Europe in conveniences and comfort in railroad traveling, as not a drink of water can be obtained on the cars. The water-closets are at stations mostly, and people must be provided with pennies. Only now and then a car with closet is to be found. Usually the train stops often for only five minutes, and passengers are all locked in the cars, the guard locking and unlocking at stations. The seats are comfortable but give me America, "the home of the brave and the land of the free."

Our ride was through a flat, rich, agricultural country. About two in the afternoon arrived in Brussels, a fine depot, where baggage had to be again examined, but owing to the experience of our courier had no trouble. Our trunks were piled on top of an hotel omnibus, heavy trunks too, and we were driven to the Grand Hotel on one of the principal streets. Have pleasant rooms facing said street, where we witness all sorts of scenes. Sunday all the stores are open, many more out than on week days; a sort of holiday; little regard for the Sabbath in continental Europe. We have driven about the city, saw the Hotel de Ville, an old building resembling a church with a tower, built in the fifteenth century, used as a town hall. Saw a wedding party enter while gazing at the building. Some of the statues on outside had some of their features worn off—noses flattened, for instance, by the ravages of time. The building had been white marble, but now nearly black with age. Not far from this hall was the famous fountain called "*Männekin Piss,*" which might shock some people, but "evil to him who evil thinks." It is said to commemorate the return of a nobleman's son who was lost. When found was in this attitude, a small boy making water; the water still flows the same as for hundreds of years. The oldest thing in Brussels, it stands against a building in a sort of a corner of a very narrow street of the fifteenth century. Many of the streets in this city are so narrow that only small carriages can pass. The sidewalks are about two feet wide. There are some broad streets in newer part of the town, and broad squares with fine fountains; an old cathedral it boasts of also. We did not visit it, but drove to the Palace of Justice, the law court, the pride of Belgium, an immense structure of white marble that consumed fifteen years in building. The French language is spoken here and French money used.

To day Mr. Spraker went to Antwerp to see an exhibition, a little more than an hour's ride by rail; returned same evening and proposed leaving at eight P.M. for Bruges, so as to travel in the cool of the day. We intended going next day, but consented to the change of time, packed hastily, donned traveling attire, dined and bade farewell to Brussels, as we thought, expecting to reach our destination about half-past ten same evening. After riding some time the train stopped, and our courier coolly informed us we were on the wrong train, and must go back to Brussels and start over again, taking another train for Ghent, which we did after some scolding of courier for the mistake, arriving about eleven o'clock P.M. We had not designed stopping here, but found the episode very novel and enjoyable. The streets on our arrival were crowded with men and women and children holding a festival or Kirmess, that had lasted four days; this was the fifth and last. The main square in centre of the town was brilliantly lighted with colored gas-jets in fancy forms; numerous bands of music and people paraded the streets, danced and drank beer without stint indoors and out. This lasted until five o'clock in the morning. After breakfast we drove about to see the queer old buildings of the fifteenth century, an old church with belfry and chimes; on top of steeple was a golden dragon said to have been brought from Church of St. Sophia, in Constantinople, to Bruges ; afterward brought to Ghent, twenty-five miles.

Later we went to Bruges, a quaint old town of the fourteenth century, a great commercial city and centre once. Its takes its name from the number of its bridges across its canals. The latter are narrow, resembling Venice, as the houses are built down to the water's edge. Visited the cathedral of the twelfth century ; saw the bronze doors, hundred of years old, in a good state of preservation ; other brass monuments in the pavement; also saw very old paintings, one of the Last Supper, Our Saviour and His Apostles, features perfect, as the coloring was also. It closed with panels ; paintings inside and outside. These panels said to have been done in the fourteenth century. In the *Hotel De Ville*, or City Hall, saw a remarkably carved wooden mantel, executed in 1529, and recently restored ; it covers nearly one side of a large room. From this place we went to Ostend, stopping at the Grand Hotel on the bank of the channel, where there is a splendid sea-wall and a remarkably fine broad promenade, that is much frequented by all classes from early morn till late at night. There are many hotels so situated at this summer resort, a "Belgian Brighton." Bathing is indulged in in a novel manner. Small houses for bathing are on wheels, and are drawn by horses to the water, as far in as the occupant desires; then drawn back again, going down a few steps into the water. Small boats are numerous and manned to render any needed assistance. A fine casino, with *cafe*, is not far from our hotel, with seats and tables, music and brilliant lights at night. To add to the attraction of this resort, King Leopold has a summer residence here, on an elevation overlooking the channel. I saw him pass by, walking with his daughter, this evening, unattended, his dress without decoration. The Belgian flag, of black, yellow and red, was flying from buildings all about; a delightfully cool summer resort. We leave in the morning for Dover, crossing the tempestuous English channel. To-night the waves are dashing and lashing themselves fearfully—a large body of water, indeed.

XI.

AGAIN IN OLD ENGLAND.

JULY 22D—We left Ostend for Dover this day, a bright ideal summer day, crossing the channel in four and a half hours. Many of the passengers were very sick; Harriet was a little sick, I none at all, avoiding it by taking a stateroom and lying down most of the time until we approached the chalk cliffs of Dover. Took luncheon in restaurant at station, waiting an hour for steamer from Calais. Then the cars whirled us at a rapid rate to London, making no stop till that city was reached. Glad were we to be again in an English speaking country, where we could understand and be understood. We took leave of our courier at Ostend, who had accompanied us for a month, a polite, convenient Frenchman, who said he should be in Paris that evening.

We are again in London, stopping at the "Langham" Hotel, a popular house for Americans. We have been making final purchases of remembrance for loved ones at home. How gladly we shall hasten to them whenever the broad

Atlantic is crossed. Have been in London nearly a week. Visited the Royal Academy, where there was, indeed, a royal collection of oil paintings—hundreds of them, and each one perfect—it would be difficult to describe them. A few that impressed me must be noticed. One was the marriage of the Duke of Albany, with Queen Victoria a central figure, with her children and grandchildren about her, all life-like and in court dress. Another was a picture of the *salon* of Madam Recamier, a beautiful lady dressed in white, after the French style of fifty years ago or more—little underclothing, displaying a graceful form. She was half reclining on a sofa, with cushions for support, the *salon* filled with notable men and women of the time, among them Madam De Stael, both literary and military celebrities, life-like likenesses of them portrayed as if in conversation. Numerous portraits were in the various rooms, admirable, of beautiful women, and faultless landscapes beside. A picture called "Gordon's Last Messenger" was memorable. A lone Turk on a dromedary, crossing a barren desert, where the bones of camels and their carcasses are scattered, made a desolate scene, but finely painted. Harriet and I were charmed.

Later, visited St. Paul's Cathedral, something

after the style of Westminister Abbey. It contains many monuments and carvings in memory of England's illustrious dead, stained-glass windows, a few oil paintings, so high in centre round the dome could not see them distinctly. We drove in a hansom a long way on the Strand to get there, one of London's busiest streets. Immense omnibuses, or "trams," as they are called here, were going back and forth, filled inside and out with living freight. Often so blocked were we that we would wait some time before we could proceed. London has a population of 5,000,000. Its suburbs extend a long way in every direction. We shopped on Regent street and in Piccadilly (does not that sound English enough?) to our hearts' content.

Upon this, a second visit to London, again visited Westminister, and must note down my impression of it. Went alone, to try and get some understanding of this wonderful structure, built six centuries ago by Henry III. Rude has been the treatment of it, yet the spires still point high to Heaven in undiminished grace, lightness, grandeur and strength. Washington Irving said, after his visit, that he endeavored to form some arrangement in his mind of the objects he had been contemplating, but found they were already fallen into indistinctness and confusion—"names, inscriptions, trophies, all become confounded in recollection, though I had scarcely taken my foot off the threshold."

So, indeed, it is a wearisome multitude of objects. If such a mind had this experience, what must it be to an ordinary one ; it was a comfort to find another had the same impression as myself. My second visit was even less satisfactory than the first. It has been said if one went daily for a year one could not see everything.

Addison says nothing else of the buried person but that he was born one day and died upon another, the whole history of his life being comprehended in those two circumstances that are common to all mankind.

I copied some of the inscriptions as follows :

" Earl of Godolphin, Lord High Treasurer of Great Britain, 1712. Monument erected by his much obliged daughter-in-law."

Major Andre's monument erected by George III. A fine monument.

One to Gen. Wolfe, who took Quebec.

Dean of Westminster, a square tomb, old gray stone, bears date 1561.

Earl and Countess of Middlesex, 1645. Two marble figures lying side by side full length, in the dress of that date, full ruff.

Epitaph : "Truly loving as truly loved wife, 1674."

Poets' Corner, so called.

Poet Chaucer, 1400.

"O Rare Ben Jonson."

Many epitaphs in Latin.

Dryden, 1700. Longfellow's bust placed here by his English admirers.

Thackeray's bust; not so prominent as Longfellow's. No inscription, only his name.

Shakespeare has a large and fine monument. Southey and Burns' busts. Samuel Johnson, LL.D., cut in pavement. David Garrick and his wife, names in pavement, raised brass letters, time of birth and death. Charles Dickens, large slab of gray marble in floor of Poets' Corner, in gilt letters; time of birth and death only.

The following epitaph was on the monument of John Gay, written by Pope:

> "Life is a jest and all things show it;
> I thought so once, now I know it."

Mrs. Scott Siddons' large monument, represents her dressed as *Lady Macbeth*. On monument of John and Charles Wesley was this: "The best of all is God with us. I look upon all the world as my parish. God buries his workmen, but carries on his work."

Before taking our final leave of London, Harriet and I took a hansom and went to Hyde Park to see the Albert Memorial, a beautiful monument erected by the Queen and her people out of love and esteem for the Prince Consort and the good he had done to the public, so stated on the monument. I was glad I did not leave before seeing it. On opposite side of the street is Albert Hall, an enormous circular building devoted to music, exhibitions of art, mechanism and all inventions. Around the dome are figures representing all kinds of industry with appropriate inscriptions. This building was erected for science and art for all nations. "Glory to God in the highest, peace on earth and good will to men." The above words are inscribed on this hall.

XII.

The Land of Burns and Scott.

July 28th.—We left London for Melrose at half-past ten A. M. on a very fast train over the midland route for Scotland; we rode through a well cultivated country; fine landscapes met our gaze; the country grew more hilly and barren as we approached Scotland. We left the English hedges, and in their place stone fences were the rule for miles and miles. Saw sheep grazing on hills so steep they could hardly keep their footing; after this rode into a better country as we draw near Melrose. We found this a quaint old town, much frequented by tourists who come to visit the Abbey, and Abbotsford, the home of Sir Walter Scott. We visited Melrose after a night's rest, finding it a ruin of the thirteenth century. Has been burnt and rebuilt, many parts of it. Last used in 1810. I gathered some wild flowers and leaves and pressed them as mementos of the visit. Melrose means rose bedecked. Took a carriage from Melrose and had a delightful drive of three miles to Abbotsford, the home of Sir Walter

Scott, now occupied by his great granddaughter; many of the rooms are thrown open to the public by paying a fee of a shilling each. You are conducted by a guide through the first-floor rooms—library, which has a flight of winding stairs to be able to reach books on high and leads to his sleeping-room, study-parlor, armory; the parlor contained portraits of the family, also a case with the clothing he last wore, even to shoes, cane, and child's silver drinking cup, his hat also.

Sir Walter Scott was born in Edinburgh in 1771; died 1832. Abbotsford is beautifully situated on the banks of the river Tweed, the house a little distance back; fine flower gardens lie between the house and river, the house on a rise of ground. Fine views are had from every window. Large trees add to the grandeur. It was said by Lord Lytton, "It is a divine pleasure to admire." We enjoyed our visit here very much, with thousands of others who have visited this place. I have some wild roses gathered from hedges on our way here which I prize.

"The City of Edinburgh, out of admiration and gratitude to Scott and his writings, which brought the history and beauty of Scotland into the prominence of these times," erected a splendid monument to his memory on Princes street, Edinburgh ; it cost 15,650 pounds sterling. The principal niches are filled with statues of his heroes and heroines. It is composed of white marble ; the outer arches resemble those of Melrose Abbey, of which Sir Walter Scott was so fond. His writings, it is admitted, gave more delight to a larger number of readers in every rank of society than any other author, save Shakespeare alone.

We arrived in Edinburgh July 29th, in the afternoon—four hundred miles from London. Scotchmen believe it the most picturesque city in the world. We, as pilgrims and strangers, agree with them in the verdict, with its hills and crags, castle and weather-stained towers and fortifications. The view from " Calton Hill " was a delight. We enjoyed it at sunset overlooking the Frith of Forth and the city below. It has been said Edinburgh is a patrician among British cities, a penniless lass with a "long pedigree." She counts great men against millionaires.

Its schools of art and universities rank high, and the citizens pride themselves on these more than manufactures or business fame. Holyrood Castle is very interesting, and historical from having been the residence of Mary Queen of Scots. Her bedroom is shown as she left it, with high-posted bedstead and the old tapestries, the coverings of bed and draperies dropping to pieces with age. Two hundred years is a long period of time. The stone stair-steps are hollowed out with use and age. Her secret stairway is shown, also Lord Darnley's rooms and the spots of blood on stairs caused by the assassination of Rizzio, an historical event. Very old paintings on the wall. The chapel attached, called the Royal Chapel, is in ruins. A beautiful fountain in the court-yard; figures sculptured thereon would do credit to any artist.

Holyrood is on low ground at one end of Edinburgh, the castle at the other. Queen Victoria has troops now stationed at Holyrood, and a notice is put up saying, that through her condescension, the historical rooms of this castle are open to the public. From Holyrood we drove through the old part of Edinburgh, which is full of historical interest—the tall peaked houses, six and seven stories high, that have been occupied in ancient times by lords and ladies, dukes and duchesses. Robert Burns is of the number of notable ones who lived here. Driving on we came to the Talbooth, made memorable by Sir Walter Scott's novel "The Heart of Midlothian." Then we came to John Knox's house, with its inscription, extending in gilt letters over nearly the entire front on first floor—a high house of several stories and peaked roof: "Lufe-God-abufe-al-and-ye-nychtbour-as-ye-self."

He lived here in 1559; a church near by is called John Knox church. The wynds, so called, are narrow streets leading off Canongate, which was the main street in olden times. The past accompanies you everywhere. This magnificent city has been styled the modern Athens. The Frith of Forth, very like the Ægean Sea, or the distant view similar. The population of Edinburgh is 227,451. The city owes its origin to the Castle rock, a military stronghold, once occupied for a brief period by the Romans. In 626 it was captured by the Saxons; it was gradually increased in size; the fortress covers seven acres of ground, 250 feet above the surrounding valley.

St. Margaret's chapel is said to be the oldest and smallest one in the kingdom, erected by Queen Margaret in the tenth century. It stands within the castle gates; the castle is used as a garrison; soldiers and ammunition plenty here; the soldiers wear red coats and green plaid trousers. The castle adds greatly to the scenery of Edinburgh. We drove on a road leading from the old town to the new, the road winding around the base of Castle hill; it was in the early evening; the castle was lighted and looked grand, " beautiful for situation " could be said of it truly. Next day we visited the castle. We were shown a small room called Queen Mary's room, where she gave birth to James the VI. Old kings dwelt in these parts. We are delighted with Edinburgh, and all that we have seen. The climate is cool even in midsummer.

To-day is my birthday, July 31, and thousands of miles separate me from home. What changes time brings! Events occur that we never dreamed of in early life. " Man proposes, God disposes." We left " Edinboro town," as the song goes, at midday; took the train for a three hours' ride through an uninteresting country, hilly, to Callander, an unimportant place; passed through Dumblane, near our stopping place. After a hasty lunch mounted with a ladder a high wagon or stage, without cover, that accommodated a dozen passengers or more; stage was drawn by four horses. Starting, we rode over hills and through vales, by the side of lochs or lakes (loch is the Scotch name for lake) nine miles, making one change, stopping at the " Trossachs," a hotel by that name, arriving at " Inversnaid," a place at the head of Lake Lomond. After leaving stage we rode twelve miles on Lake or Loch Katrine. Rob Roy was the name of the small steamer, this being the neighborhood of Rob Roy's exploits. We remained over night at Inversnaid, dining and breakfasting here—a well kept hotel, beautiful and romantic spot. An old-fashioned garden, filled with vegetables and flowers, after the style of my grandfather's garden when I was a child ; woods and waterfall ; in background mountain and lake scenery—Loch Lomond and Ben Lomond—the former the lake, the other mountain of that name.

We rode twenty-five miles by steamer on this lake in the morning, arriving at a small place at end of the lake, where we took train for an hour's ride to Glasgow, which city, after looking about, taking a long walk, etc., we have decided against, having seen more drunkenness and vagrancy than in any city yet visited. We leave to-night after an hour's ride, take steamer for Belfast, Ireland, across the Irish sea or channel. We do this at night, thus hoping to avoid sea-sickness and discomfort.

XIII.

"The Ould Sod."

We arrived in Belfast early Sunday morning, August 2d, a dull, dark day. The city looked solemn, with its gray, smoky stone buildings and large linen warehouses. In the afternoon took a carriage ride about the town for two hours; went to the outskirts. It is the second city in Ireland; saw caves in the mountains or the dark entrances thereto; the giant's ring where a battle had been fought in ye olden time. We were little interested in this. Put up at the "Imperial Hotel." In Belfast, were not made very comfortable. Late in the day took train for five hours' ride, including many stops, making it rather tedious, though we saw the famous peat bogs of Ireland, the low, one-storied cottages of the poor, whitewashed and looking neat, yet so small they bore little trace of comfort. The land looked poor; some fields of grain and flax were being harvested; have not found linen very abundant or cheap in Dublin whence we came from Belfast. Drove a long way in Phœnix Park; contains 1,750 acres of ground, fine large trees, with herds of cows and deer in large numbers grazing there. Fine roads, too, zoological and flower gardens at different entrances to the Park.

The chief objects of interest in Dublin are Trinity College, Nelson's Monument, and those to O'Connell and other notables. The city is situated on a bay of same name; the city is divided by the river Liffey, and connected by fine substantial bridges, like many of the European cities. Saw the residence of the Lord Lieutenant, near the Park. Streets broad, and plenty of soldiers, English, Scotch and red coats. Life size statues of Goldsmith and Burke stand on either side of entrance to Trinity College—these men were students there. Weather rainy and uncomfortably cool; thermometer stands at 58 degrees.

AUGUST 5TH.—Left Dublin by rail; a dark, cool, rainy day; could hardly keep comfortable in cars; over one hundred miles distant to Killarney, whither we are bound, through a poor country, peat bogs, and occasionally a small cottage of one story, goats, cows, and flocks of geese in the meadows. The country mostly level and swampy, the pink heather in blossom here and there, till we drew near Killarney, when high hills or mountains diversified the scenery. A sudden curve in the road brought us to the desired station. Hotel porters and omnibuses seemed to indicate quite a town. We were recommended to the "Royal" as a stopping-place, so seated ourselves in omnibus belonging thereto, which was soon filled with passengers, thus proving its popularity. We were driven through the village, composed of one long street, with small stores on either side. I have never seen so many dirty, barefooted women together before. On every street corner stood a slovenly woman, with her child in arms, a shawl wrapped about them both; poor and dirty was the average. We drove for two miles, I should think, through highways and woods to our hotel, which stands in an open space a short distance from Lake Killarney, so celebrated in song as the home of Kate Karney. The lakes are picturesque, with islands and row-boats, the mountains towering up from the lakes, three in number, one five miles long, one two and a half miles. Row-boats alone are used for excursions.

I am too anxious to get home, now that our tour is nearly finished by land. One week more before embarking on "City of Rome" for New York. I must confess to a feeling of homesickness and impatience for the happy day when we shall begin our ocean ride, still more so for the termination of it. May a kind and watchful Providence guide our ship and favor us with fair weather and a pleasant passage to our beloved land and home, sweet home.

Harriet, James and I took a row on Lake Killarney; enjoyed it too. The sun came out brightly; later it rained, as it does very often in Ireland, the Emerald Isle, a name given in consequence of this, possibly. The oarsman, a typical Irishman, entertained us with legends of the shore and rocks. We saw ruins of castle and monastery of the early centuries; altogether had a pleasant afternoon. The three lakes and connecting rivers extend a distance of fifteen miles.

The days are gradually passing; time, like an ever rolling flood, is bearing us on; just now it cannot pass too quickly, as I am so anxious to start for home and America. Three months seem a long time to be wandering through strange lands. We sometimes find a hotel that we like and are made comfortable in, though seldom, yet have patronized the best recommended in every city. Shall appreciate home the more for our experience.

It has been said of going from home, that it would be far less pleasant to go if one had nothing to leave, therefore nothing to regret. What a mockery would that going be, with nothing to return to with joy; no one to listen and sympathize and wonder at the recital of adventure and experience! This gives zest to one's return. I hope our experience will be profitable in knowledge of foreign countries and customs, of which we have read and talked all our lives and of knowing by separation from family and home how to appreciate both. How blest I am and how dear they are to me!

Harriet and I came on to the City of Cork from Killarney alone, as James took a stage ride of forty miles by another route, to see the country and its inhabitants in their everyday life and state. He will join us to-day. We expect to spend Sunday here in Cork; it seems to be a lively commercial city, situated on bay of same name; the river Lee divides it; good substantial bridges. The city is very dirty; ragged, barefooted, desolate women and girls beg in the street bareheaded, sights that are never seen in cities of the New World. We remained in Cork from Friday until the following Monday. Found our hotel, the "Imperial," quite poor—the name to the contrary; it was old and poorly kept. So were glad to bid adieu to both hotel and city. The morning we left was showery, yet we took landau and drove to the famous Blarney Castle, a distance of six miles through the college grounds. A fine building, (the college), of two hundred years old, built on the banks of the river Lee. We passed by fine fields of grain, large trees, etc., a much pleasanter outlook than the city itself. Blarney Castle is a ruin now; but little left of it save the tall tower. One hundred and eighty steps take you to the top of tower, where the Blarney stone is secured by two iron bands, and to kiss it one must be held over it. Though a dangerous experience, the attendant said it was done daily. The tradition is, that kissing it will make one forever eloquent and smooth-tongued.

Blarney Castle was built in 1440, by the McCarthy; walls and tower fourteen feet thick; the castle and surrounding acres are owned by a gentleman who resides near the castle; land well cultivated. We left Cork by rail, though small steamers run several times a day on the river Lee that connects Cork with Queenstown, a distance of eleven miles. We came to Queenstown to await the arrival of the steamship "City of Rome," which we expect on the morning of the 13th, at 7 o'clock, so we are getting everything in readiness to-day with hearts full of expectation and anticipation of being at home in a few days.

We are stopping at the Queen Hotel, facing the harbor, a poor hotel, though considered the best here, a poor compliment to her Majesty—poor cuisine, the house dirty and old. Queenstown is finely situated, a maratime city, one of the best harbors in the world, ten miles square; ships from all parts of the world lay at anchor here awaiting orders from Liverpool, etc. Poor shops line the main street, dirty women as hucksters and little of interest save the shipping and fine harbor. We took a drive in a jaunting-car, a kind of conveyance only known in Ireland, and drove fourteen miles into the country. Fine roads and views all the way being on high ground; the road often lay between rows of trees that met overhead, forming an arch; ripe fields of grain, land mostly owned by one or two gentlemen, a thatched cottage here and there and ruins of the tenth century, added to the interest of the drive. Had a pleasant afternoon, helping to divert us while waiting. We found the country far more attractive than the town.

At length the delightful day dawned when we were to embark for the homeward trip. Time is said to be the devourer of all things, but the last few days seemed interminable; have hardly known how to employ ourselves, being really homesick;

the weather, too, has been dark and dreary, rain descending about two-thirds of the year in Ireland, we were told. We rose early and were on the deck of the " tender," a small steamer without covering for our heads in either rain or sun; were packed in on deck with crowds of emigrants and their friends who were escorting them to the steamer bound for America. We did not blame them for leaving " Ould Ireland," a poverty-stricken country—uninviting and homeless. We traveled in the east and central and southern parts; saw little but dirt and poverty; no thrift or enterprise; am told by travelers that the northern portion is better, more industry, and the Protestant religion prevails.

XIV.

HOMEWARD BOUND.

The morning sun shone brightly, and we thought ourselves highly favored for sailing day, not having enjoyed a bright day for a week. But with delay of loading, etc., it was nine o'clock before the "City of Rome" was reached, lying outside Queenstown harbor. The ship had left Liverpool the afternoon before, a distance of 220 miles. Once on board, she soon started with so little noise or motion we were hardly aware of it, being engaged in breakfasting. It seemed like meeting an old friend to be on board the steamship again—occupying same staterooms, meeting Captain Munro, attendants, etc., etc. Knowing we were homeward-bound, were happy. A little rain fell before we left the tender, and dark lowering weather succeeded for days.

After lunch Harriet and I began to experience seasickness, so retired to our staterooms. This was Thursday. Were not able to go to the dining-room again for some time. On Sunday were able to be up all day for the first. I attended the religious services held in the dining-room, which was well filled. The services consisted of an organ recital, a solo by a lady—"The Lord is my Shepherd"—prayer, thanking the good Lord for having given us a prosperous voyage and imploring safety for the rest of the journey; a short address or sermon from the Gospel of John, 1st chapter, "Follow thou me" being the subject; singing concluded the devotions. About noon a fog and misty rain began, and the hoarse sound of the foghorn was heard at short intervals, all the afternoon and night, keeping me awake, as there seemed danger on the deep, and we were approaching the banks of Newfoundland.

I trusted in kind Providence that had watched over and guided us through dangers, seen and unseen, and kept us safely. We have made a good run, to use a sailing phrase, of four hundred miles and more every day. Copy of time made in passage: August 13th and 14th part of each day, 452 miles; 15th, 418 miles; 16th, 428 miles; 17th, 400 miles; 18th, 434 miles; 19th, 409 miles.

AUGUST 17TH.—This morning we had a rain storm, high seas, so the ship rolled and the water dashed furiously over the portholes. I rose and dressed, but was very soon compelled to undress, retire to berth and pay tribute to old Neptune, and remained quiet until late in the afternoon, when the storm abated, the sea calmed (my stomach also).

Harriet and I dressed hastily, went on deck, and dined there in our steamer chairs. During the afternoon we sailed within two miles of the shores of Newfoundland, saw the green grass and hills for many miles. A telegraph station was signaled, messages sent to New York and England of the " City of Rome's " whereabouts, only four days out of sight of land ; it was told us that it was rare that a vessel approaches so near the shores. There are all sorts of speculations regarding the time of our arrival at Sandy Hook among the passengers to-day ; the Captain promises Thursday, at six in the morning ; we are so impatient to meet friends we can scarcely wait.

AUGUST 19TH.—Last night, after retiring at eleven o'clock, the engine ceased its motion and many were apprehensive of danger. I looked out of the porthole immediately, when I saw a sail-boat of good size with bright lights aloft, and a row-boat at side of the ship ; found in the morning it was a pilot-boat and a pilot was taken on board. At noon to-day we had traveled 409 miles during the last twenty-four hours ; we are at 1 o'clock 265 miles from Sandy Hook, and are promised sight of land at midnight, so shall breakfast in New York to-morrow, Providence permitting. Last evening a concert was given, or an entertainment, that is customary on every trip of an ocean steamer for the Mariners' Hospital in Liverpool; only forty-five dollars were contributed, less than the usual amount; there was little talent either in a musical way or in recitations.

We have had a thunder shower this afternoon that drove many from the deck, where the air is delightfully cool; have had fog, too, so that the booming of the fog-horn was heard for a little while.

We are hastening on to port and friends after a long absence; cannot get there too soon for an impatient party like ourselves. The afternoon cleared off beautifully, fine breeze, and have seen whales, several of them, spouting in the waves; one so far forgot his dignity as to jump partly out of the water, far enough to reveal his size and dark color, causing great excitement among the three hundred passengers on board. We have not had a whole day of sunshine and brightness on this trip. It is now certain that the ship will be sighted at Fire Island, the nearest point of land, where news of the arrival of the ship can be reported to

New York, at midnight to-night, then two or three hours more before Sandy Hook is reached.

Mark Twain says " that only those natures made up of pluck and endurance, devotion to duty for duty's sake, and invincible determination, may hope to venture upon so tremendous an enterprise as keeping a journal and not sustain a shameful defeat." Having accomplished this enterprise, may I not lay claim to some of the above qualities in a small degree.

XV.

At Last, Home, Sweet Home.

A night of almost entire wakefulness was passed, keeping watch to see the first glimmer of light from the land ; the night seemed long, the water deep and dark. After frequent visits to the port-hole, about two o'clock in the morning a row of lights greeted my eyes: the engines were still, and I knew there would be nothing to expect till morn, so resigned myself to a few hours of sleep, but arose early and was dressed and on the lookout for a steamboat with the Star-in signal, bearing what members of the family were in the city, to meet us: and we were not disappointed, for my husband, with my sons Charles and Howard and others, had lodged upon one of his steamboats near by all night, waiting for the arrival of the "City of Rome." We were soon transferred with our baggage to the Starin boat and soon reached the Barge Office.

After duly passing through the Custom-house, Charles, Harriet and I took a carriage and drove to 9 West Thirty-eighth street, where my husband joined us. New York looked very new after our visit to the Old World, but so bright and homelike, we were so delighted to be again upon our native land and with our own dear ones. We took an afternoon train for Starin Place, Fultonville, where my mother was; Caroline, and her boys, as well as Harriet's children, were there —Myndert was also. On arrival at Fonda Station quite a party of friends met us, and approaching Starin Place we found it illuminated from base to tower in honor of our coming; a long table prepared for supper, and floral pieces in every room, symbolical of the event, and "joy was unconfined" this evening and the next day, when the presents we had brought for the children, young and old, were unpacked. Such a happy day is beyond description and one long to be remembered, so much to hear on every side. The delight of being a reunited family was unlimited.

Home, sweet, sweet home, and all the dearer for our wanderings, was found at last. So we went through, and so ended our trip to Europe. To this day I cherish it as among the most gratifying memories of my life. And, as I said in the beginning, if in living with me over again some of the scenes and incidents of our journey, my husband, children and friends, for whom this little book is intended, find pleasure or profit; then the labor of preparing it has been more than repaid.

LAURA M. STARIN.

www.ingramcontent.com/pod-product-compliance
Lightning Source LLC
Chambersburg PA
CBHW020858160426
43192CB00007B/976